A Baker's Nickel

ALSO BY WILLIAM S. COHEN

Of Sons and Seasons (poetry), 1978
Roll Call, 1981
Getting the Most Out of Washington, 1982
The Double Man (a novel with Gary Hart), 1985

A Baker's Nickel

Poetry by
William S. Cohen

William Morrow and Company, Inc.
New York

Library of Congress Cataloging-in-Publication Data

Cohen, William S.
A baker's nickel.

I. Title.
PS3553.0434B34   1986   811'.54   86-8409
        ISBN 0-688-65449-X

Printed in the United States of America

First Edition

1 2 3 4 5 6 7 8 9 10

For Harry Cohen, whose courage carried him from Bialystock to Bangor,

and

for his son, Reuben, who at seventy-seven still kicks the devil from his door.

Foreword

SOMETIMES A PHRASE, a fleeting melody, a scent or
sound prompts me to pick up my pen and start writ-
ing. There is never a prearranged time during which
I stare at a blank page until thoughts are transcribed
into words. For me, it's almost always a random ex-
perience and very nearly a spiritual one.

I have always been fascinated by words: how their
tone and texture fall upon the inner ear; how awk-
ward some look upon the page; how musical they can
be when arranged just so. For more than twenty-five
years I have known the exquisite joy of constructing
small mosaics, which reflect events and moods that
remain so selectively special. I have carried them around
in an old folder that I occasionally turn to when there
is the need to escape the incessant chatter that fills
much of my daily occupation.

The poems that have been included in this volume
span that quarter century. They have not been dated
as I prefer to think that the relative age of the author
did not influence the experience or the need to de-
scribe it.

As with *Of Sons and Seasons*, I have added some
introductory thoughts to certain poems with the hope
that their context might enhance, rather than explain,
their meaning.

Contents

The purpose of poetry is to remind us
how difficult it is to remain just one person,
for our house is open, there are no keys in the doors
and invisible guests come in and out at will.

—CZESLAW MILOSZ
Bells in Winter

Part One

$\mathcal{M}$Y GRANDFATHER died when I was ten years old. His name was Harry.

Harry was one of the thousands who fled Russia around the turn of the century, stepped on a crowded boat and headed for America, where he hoped to begin a new life.

He changed his surname to Cohen somewhere between Bialystok (now part of Poland) and Ellis Island. I did not know much about him. Did he cross Europe on foot? What was it like for him to be on the boat or in New York City without a kopeck or a penny? What drew him north to Boston, finally to Bangor, Maine? What pulled him to the dough bins of a bakery? All remains a mystery to me.

I remember how he used to walk slowly from the tenement house in which we lived on Hancock Street three hundred yards down the street to the Bangor Rye Bread Company where he, his two sons, daughter and my mother baked and delivered the best bread "north of Boston." During his final years, his existence was defined by that linear distance between home and workplace, much as my father's is even now.

The only thing we shared during my childhood was the soup that my aunt Gittle used to make each day for him and my exchange of gratitude for an Indian-headed nickel, an exchange which became a weekly ritual.

Grandfather Talk

Are our grandfathers
ever so wise and majestic
as mahogany clocks

That stand tall,
tocking away in all
the living rooms
of dying time?

Mine was old and bent
who shuffled with pain
into his final days.

A gentle man
whose hands (like my father's)
were strong and flour-caked,

Who looked at me
with great sad eyes
as he, a baker man, handed me
a white-dusted nickel
for the week.

"Some day, Billy, someday
you will understand"
were the only words
he ever spoke or those
I can recall

Words that taunt
me even now
as a grandfather clock
swings its tongue
in syncopated talk

And I keep waiting
for the meaning.

Song or Epitaph

Come in to the dark
where the clock
does not govern,

Here, where the
blacktop stops
and briars erect
a barricade.

Embrace a world
of wilderness
where children
walk on fours,

And birches bend,
beautiful and white,

Where red needles and
perfectly cast cones
lie on a carpet of moss
that softens the fall
of pines grown old,

Tall warriors that
need no burial,
wooden bones that
wither into
dust.

Here, if you cared,
you could write
a song—or an
epitaph.

Spring Run

Leaning into a March
wind, warm before
its time,

I catch the song
of spring, bouncing
on branches in
loud delirium.

Their flutes buried
in their bursting throats,
the feathered musicians
celebrate the death
of winter's cold kiss
and touch the lips
of a new sun that
sends ice melting
into nothingness.

Out here, out on the highway
where minutes turn to miles,
where faceless cars pass by
blind in their very speed,
I run, not for glory or for deed,
but for me, a race
against my heart
that pounds like an
angry fist in the
midnight of its cage.

I kick on,
trying to beat time
in some desperate kind
of rage,

Until I am free,
free of fatigue, of pain
of breathlessness, and I
can even see
the course of blood
sprinting through a
network of veins and arteries

For one fleeting moment
leaning into the morning light,
beyond all fear
I am part of the trees,
the birds, the warm wind,
the water running
into the glory of green,

I am spring
in the summer of
my years.

Dylan

Thirty years since
a poet passed, slipped
unnoticed by most into night,
a candlelight that flickered
out and into darkness.

Word mania seized him no more,
no madness to compel
a taking up of the penknife
to carve from his soul
soothing syllables
into a meaning
beyond all that we see.

No lying in state,
no riderless black horse
bearing empty leather boots
honored the silencing
of his lips
the congealing of his eye.

Oh, boy of summer
who played to ruin
in the mustard-seed sun
that was once young
for you,

Who carried morning songs
in apple carts, strewing
them as seeds in fields
gone brown, heedless,
lusty, burning down
all the windblown way
brandied into roof-high hay.

I sit and listen
to the sea waves
wash against the
salt-worn rocks.
And I see you
still green, still golden,
still singing in your chains.

To Look Back

To look back
might mean never
to go on.

To see the pile
of shattered glass
and broken days,
the horror of
time that's lost.

To listen for
the voices of sons
that ran once
like laughing brooks,

To hear the echo
of footfalls when
they walked into
mustaches and manhood
before I turned.

If I should thumb
through photographs that
remind me how I've
lived in the margins
of my life,

I might never go on,
climbing Jacob's mystic ladder
into the night,
searching for a place
to rest in some
perfect light.

I might stop.

And what then?

Part Two

Part Two

Behind My Eyes

How light is your touch?

Light as the lash
that seals the eye,

Soft as star codes
that blink and cry
in the cold universe.

Have you ever heard
the mesh of two
fingertips between
the scented silk
of night?

Or the sinking of oil
into grain of solid wood,
the scream of phantoms
inside of dreams,
the running of September
red into apple skins?

I sit here on the quiet
corner of my thoughts
while jet engines whisper
into the Atlantic's ice-blue
ear

And I hear your lips
unfold like blood-red
flowers in the dark—

love shadows hanging
light in my heart.

There will be time enough
for momentary connections
minutes from now
when I will ride
a painted horse in a carrousel
waving, smiling to all
the first name faces
that will blur and go blank
as the pages in my hands.

To hold this hour,
before the brilliant blue
of the morning
breaks into sand
and runs to dusk,

Now, before I touch
the sun and fall
into the sea,

Come lie with me,
here in the darkness
behind the shades
that hide my eyes.

Fingerprints

Let me touch you,
gently, as the artist
strokes his canvas
with the whisper
of his brush.

Let me trace your hair,
lightly, with fingertips
so you can sense,
then just feel
the winding path
of my flesh's prints.

Let me look into your eyes,
softly, so that my thoughts
sink through and drop
deep into your heart
yet make no rings.

Let me linger here,
weightless, upon this moment
before a breeze comes up
unannounced and scatters
my words like so many leaves
in autumn.

Hidden Galaxies

I dreamed I stood
upon a star
and found a path
to all of the heaven's
hidden galaxies.

And there I walked
along the rim
of endless nights
and vast eternities,

Searching for some sign,
some clue to you
embedded in the
silver dust,

Calling out your name
in vain along the valleys
of the lost.

Suddenly, I saw
your eyes glowing
in the dark.

They beckoned me
to kiss your lips
and caress your
golden head.

But just as I
reached out to
touch your face
and take you
into my embrace,
you closed your eyes
and disappeared.

I screamed a silent scream
that shattered the
night's cold crystal
and echoed into
empty years.

Then I awoke and saw you
lying next to me,
turning in your beauty
sighing in your sleep.

Night Verse

How can I show
my love?

Wild flowers picked
from a dark forest,

A bucket full of butterflies
gathered from a perfumed field?

Shall I trace
your face among the stars
and pray you will not
fall beyond the
reach of Orion?

Shall I ask
the rain to dance
a minuet with
the sun, while
I pluck at the plum
of your lips?

Gently, I sing my verses,
soundless, the way
fog touches the wing
of a nightbird

Until
I reach and enter
that open-doored dream,
the place where you
first touched me
and left me with
this infinite wound.

Secret Harbor

Years lie like roses
　　strewn across
　　our youth.

In their lightness
　　the being of beauty
　　still sings in eyes
　　that hide the mysteries
　　of lives past due.

Were you she-lion?
Pioneer or queen?

The veil drops,
　　the secrets remain.
　　O, the lightness
　　of the lash.

Your face,
　　anointed
　　by light that spills
　　its smile
　　across waters that
　　show each shade
　　of green and blue,
　　blues that bruise
　　the heart.

As the sun sinks
　　by minutes to its death,

Burning every cloud
　　emerald to amber
　　in its long cry.

Pine trees, straight
　　as truth, watch
　　the ceremony
　　unfold.

As stars blink
    to life, assuming
    their title to the
    night.

The winds go calm,
    all motion sits poised
    on a sudden
    intensity,

A stillness
    pure as a hand
    plucking a string of silk
    begins to sing

And in that silent song
    I am wounded
    with the ecstasy
    of a peace
    too perfect to be
    but for eternity.

It is gone now,
    all but the memory
    that lingers softer
    than the lap of
    lake water against
    the moon.

The rush of the day
    returns.

Time chases after us
    and we run like
    children against the wind.

Ahead of it for now.

Part Three

Our sons, Kevin and Christopher, are young adults now. Time has been at once kind and cruel. The nest has emptied too soon and we are left to observe their pursuits and experiences from a distance.

For many years, I tried to capture their essence, to hold back the hour hands of the clock with words. It was a futile gesture. I felt like Sisyphus with his rock. They changed almost by the day, and what I caught was a moment as evanescent as a snowflake in the palm of a warm hand.

Second Born

Christopher, second-born son of
mine,
no sacrifice to a bush-burning god
shall I make of you,
no wool-headed testament of love
to a mountain echo
that comes to biblical men
in unwitnessed dreams.

You lay buried, a miniature bone,
long before Cain, on the bottom
of some silent sea
until stirred one night
by two lovers locked
in a wave of sighs.

Then, while twisting toward
your silted bed,
a tide caught and pulled
you into a slow liquid journey
to an unknown land
and spewed you on our shore
naked and white
in the surf and sand.

You are here now,
carved by the slow
friction of time,
a boy in the image
of man.

And to you I sing this praise,
puffed up and swollen with pride,
because you are you
and yes, a child of mine,
and the wagging tongues
of wordless men shall never
diminish your place in my eyes.

You are all poise and courage
bursting from room to room
in paper helmet and wooden sword
slaying imaginary dragons
or mid-morning burglars,
but tender enough too
to fall broken and undone
if struck with the hand
of an unkind word.

All men sing the glory
of their sons. So I sing
to you. But I praise
too the man and woman
who broke your sleep
in their bruised bed,
and breathed light
into your eyes
with the kiss of love.

No Definition

Christopher, you are
a geometry of crystals,
a white prism that
bends the light
into rainbows, a complex
of color that blinds
me blue.

I see your gold
but cannot touch
you with my words
that whirl and sink
into italics that do not
define your second and
third meanings.

Leprechauns reside in your eyes.
They leap out onto pages
and run into penciled designs.
An artist's touch emerges.
I've caught you, I think,
and then you shift
and ride some roaring
machine across pathless fields,
fearless, the wind in your hair,
or barrel down an ice-crazed
mountain trail on the fiber-glass
edge of control, the leprechauns
just laugh and jump back.

You retreat into solitude,
carving wood, bending steel
into tools, alone with
your thoughts, patient
as the leaf that waits
for the sun to raise
the water heat into buds,
then bloom.

You are fire, flickering
green and blue, dropping
red into feather-light coals,
bursting again into a yellow
roar.

You are essence,
I conclude, an intelligence
that burns into words
that need no definition.

Kevin

Time falls, wheat shafts
under the scythe,
days lie in sheaths
of yellow gold
of deeds done,
not done, there
is no sound.

Silence, if you
listen long enough,
becomes a sound
that sings into
tissue and scars,

Stars shift in the night,
earth spins on its
perfect incline,
there is no grind,
no tick of time,
only silence as bones
stretch, night stalks,
moon white and arch
toward some final form
undefined for now.

Dreams float like
dark loam on my mind
and I see you
at seventeen,
an echo of my youth,
rippling out, sea waves,
sound swirls, shimmering
golden in the sun.

My prayers are parsed
without accent into a
savage sort of rhyme.

I watch you turn
in the membrane
of your sleep,
a flutter of infinity
roars in my ears
but makes no sound.

I wonder
does my father
stand mute
in his flour-filled days
that shrink to their
cosmic conclusion

and hear this drip
of the universe?

A Birthday

We come again
to that light
curve of Time

That marks
the primordial spark
of birth,

When you emerged
from the fluid
womb of night

Into the light
of our lives.

The cycle of seasons
has come and gone
as the sun comes

Silently over the horizon
breaking bright as blood,
then blooming
then folding
then dark.

Time does not stop.

Perhaps I should impart
some cosmic reason

Why seven years
have slipped by
since I last picked
up my pen.

Seven years of feast
seven years of famine
seven days a week.

Seven years since
you were eight.

You are no longer a boy,
but stand poised
on the rim
of manhood.

Tall, tender.

Sure but unsure.
Growing, reaching,
searching for Self.

On the edge
of the earth's paradox,
imponderables hang
in elliptical thoughts,

And I still marvel
at the mystery and mercy
of it all.

Part Four

*A*s a member of the Senate Armed Services Committee, I have the opportunity to visit our soldiers in the field and our sailors at sea.

In the spring of 1980, at the urging of my friend Captain John McCain (now a congressman), I traveled to Luke Air Force Base in Arizona to fly in the F-15, perhaps our best all-purpose combat aircraft. After a large breakfast, and a mercifully short briefing on the procedures for ejecting from the aircraft, I found myself blazing down the runway and then rocketing up toward the sun, reaching an altitude of sixteen thousand feet in less than sixty seconds.

It was an extraordinary experience and a humbling one. For nearly an hour, Captain Conley Bradford put the Eagle through aerobatic exercises that, at once, exhilarated and terrified me. Gravity took the form of an invisible monster that seemed bent upon altering my skeletal system.

I have flown on other fighter aircraft on a number of occasions since that time, but nothing quite measures up to that first experience of fear masquerading as fun.

Flight of the Eagle

(For Capt. Conley Bradford)

The blood rushed
down, pulled into
the bone bulb
of spine by
gravity's heavy
hand.

Vast, green-brown land
shrinking to square
quilts of soil,
sewn, it seemed,
by iron-lunged
machines.

And then, the sun
breaking into golden beads
as we burst into
the blue eye of
God.

A burn shot.
Straight up, a
bowel-breaking
thrust through the
cloud-scattered skies,

The roll left,
a momentary hover,
and then the dive,
a glide, graceful and gentle
as a blessing.

High over the Arizona desert
and the great red gorge
we roared, wings swept,
talons tucked, racing sound,
seconds ahead of the thunder-
clap
of Time.

We stick-rolled the
horizon on its head
and played with forces
that touched our bones
with lead.

We were quicksilver
sliding on the blue
water of thought,
unmindful, almost, that
on the gleaming wings
of the death machine
hung the terrible paradox
of peace.

For one hour,
I was fused with
beauty, violence and power,

And a sense of the holy.

High Frontier

Satellites fly,
Frankenstein birds
with burning eyes
that shutter click
into the vast night,

Out in the trackless void
they scan the earth
searching for prey
to catch on film
then let drop
down through the long
darkness, tumbling
toward the sea.

Now, nightbirds,
(gods that we are)
it is time
you were given talons
to hold these
mother-of-pearl pistols

So when the earth
goes red with a
thousand suns, you can
fire your light
into the breast of sky
a thousand times, star-drilled
into all the hydrogen-headed
monsters that rise up
from earth and sea
contemplating great
catastrophe.

Before they unleash
hurricane winds,
Before they breathe
through nostrils red
beyond all Fahrenheit,
Turn them to endless
ash, yes, save us from
their savagery.

Oh, watchful
birds of peace
happy in your
lonely epicycles,

Did you always think
you would be free
from violence, that
the night would be
only for you,
a wildlife refuge,
a cold dark silence?

Apple III

The world spins,
turning in the night's silence,
its grind, the sound of light,
heard by stars that
hang mute on
their cold hibernation

Earth, wind and water
elements fused by fire
into centuries of shining hours
measured by the hand
of God.

The Apple,
more than fruit now,
brings us mere facts
faster, while wisdom
still wanders blind
in the desert heat.

Oh, Adam,
did temptation
bring us to a
final judgment
that rests under the
palsied fingers of old men,

Sons of Cain, barking
ideologies from dry throats
into straw-stuffed ears?

What metaphysic
is this,

That we, turning
in the darkness
of the hour,
should return
on the wings of science
to a garden of
nothingness?

The Choice

Suppose the line clicked dead
and no voices screaming
"STOP, it's a mistake!"
could be fed to foreign ears?

Suppose the heavens
opened up and a rain
of missiles fell on earth
and strung a chain of neutrons
into the horror of every war
and the roar was louder
than the cries of every man
that ever died with a bullet
or bayonet in his throat,

And all the blood that
had ever spilled and stained
the earth was boiled
in one atomic vat?

Suppose the earth
became a ball of sun
and flamed until it
cindered into dust,

And laughter cracked
across the universe
as evil did rejoice?

Would God conclude
that His mistake
was giving man the choice?

Here we lie because we did not choose
To shame the land from which we sprung.
Life, to be sure, is nothing much to lose,
But young men think it is, and we were young.
—A. E. HOUSEMAN

"Don't make war bigger than life because it's not bigger than death. And
remember, at the end of every bullet, someone's son is dying."
—JOHN FITZSIMMONS
(Spoken at the Vietnam Veterans Memorial dedication in
Augusta, Maine)

D OUBTS ABOUT Vietnam still cut through our lives
and literature. Who lost the war—the military? the
media? the politicians? Was it the lack of will or the
absence of wisdom? Were the dominoes real and worth
dying for in any case? These questions need to be
asked even if they might never be resolved, for we
have the power to profit from our past.

December 26, 1983 remains a special day for me.
The day before, our family had celebrated Christmas
with opening of gifts, eating of turkey, drinking of
wine. We were together with our sons, who then were
rapidly approaching adulthood. My wife, Diana, and
I felt it was important to remind them (and ourselves)
that our nation was at peace and we were free. But
there were families for whom such holiday celebra-
tions would always mean empty chairs and haunting
memories.

We went to visit the Vietnam War Memorial in

Washington. I wanted to find and touch the name of Allen Loane, a friend who had played guard with me on the Bowdoin College basketball team. One summer I walked over 650 miles through the state of Maine, but I never walked farther or felt more exhausted than I did that day. I found Allen's name buried in a mass grave of black marble. For a long time, I just stared at it and the names of the other boys (their average age was nineteen) who died because they were brave and believed in their country. We hugged our sons. And then the tears came.

Descent

i

The memorial is cut
below grade, brutal
and sharp as a knife
wound into the earth.

It is V-notched and black,
like the night,
like the memory,
like death's foul breath.

By design
I must descend
progressively deeper
into the hell
of all the names
that come like a blizzard
of blood, the names
no longer just numbers,
but mind-numbing names
that sing of America,
of young men who
once lived and laughed,
who broke and bled
into blackness.

Etched into the mirrored marble
the names come at random,
not by alphabet, but
by the tick of tragedy,
the booby trap of time.

And I am but one
who carries out
the long body count.

Others come,
parents bent with grief,
Veterans, some with
twisted or severed limbs,
strangers, too, wearing faces
white and grim.

All are amputees of sorts
who know the phantom pain
of something vital
that's been lost.

The circle of agony
grows wide as water
broken by fifty-six
thousand rocks.

ii

For years,
    I tried to forget
that you died. The
memories of our days
as T-shirted warriors,
of balls we bounced
on wooden floors
in a conflict of a happy
kind, I let drop,
old rags into blind
emptiness.

I remember reading
(almost by accident)
that after the wound
came meningitis; like
an army of white lice
they invaded your spine
and chewed your soul.

So long
you remained a dust-
covered dream, a dream
of darkness where your face
never quite took shape
or floated into full view
before falling away,
and your final agonies
made no sound more
than pine trees moving
in the night wind.

iii

Vietnam,
a tortured slice of land
brought once into
living-room range,
but not near enough
for us to know the terror
of nightfall, of the coming
of assassins, of knives razored
for throats, of land laced
with dynamite, of children
wrapped tight with smiles
ready to explode. . . .

None of us knew
the final terror of not
knowing quite why,
why in the darkness
(spinning out abstractions of
peace)
you had to wait
the coming of death.

As I pass this
mass grave of names,
searching longitude and
latitude lines—as if
you were a piece of geography—
I come closer to the horror,
to the pain, but no closer
to the answer.

I look through salt-filmed eyes
into the question mark faces
of my sons and can
say only that I knew
you once—when we
were twenty and innocent.

Eye of Paradox

How is it
that midnight sometimes
comes to me
in the blazing light
of noon?

That an evening owl
perches on my mind,
cooing to the sun
as if a quarter moon?

Why is it
that I am struck
by night as morning
strikes its golden tongue
against the bruised bell
of Time,

And in the very
midst of joy
I can hear
the echoes of
my father's futile run
against the cruel
slanting of the sun?

Perhaps mine's a mind
half innocent, half blind,
at odds with the
human circumstance;

Perhaps it's that
in the attic
of my youth
I once saw an old
and battered box,

And found inside
neither secret nor surprise
but the blinking eye
of paradox.

Part Five

Anonymous

Soaring in a silver cylinder
high above clouds
that hang like metaphysics
behind my eyes,

I clutch in the corner
one hour of solitude,
of solitariness that stretches
like a vein between
patience and pain
into my mind.

A sound.
     Is it Poe's raven
that sits on my shoulder
tapping gently on my thoughts?

I turn to catch only a
stranger's
furtive glance that awaits
some word of recognition.

I slip by his eyes,
back to a folder of papers
that have gone blank
in the blinding light
of the morning sun.

Free Fall

Passenger again on a plane,
Heading for Maine. A flying bus
Crammed with strangers,
Faces humid in the summer air
Marked with a quiet kind
Of despair.

I watch them and wonder
Whether their thoughts pound
Against the bone cage of brain,
Do they give themselves without thought
To the care of a faceless captain
Who, if he errs (perhaps is
Only blinded by a fog bank)
Takes us into a salt-washed seawall?

Did a mechanic, laced with lassitude,
A late-night indulgence, lose
In the grayline of bolts
A checkpoint, a turn of screw?

"Delta's ready when you are."
But am I ready?

The roar of engines drowns
The whisper in my ear.
I cannot hear, therefore,
Cannot think—or be—
But a passenger in this
Silver-packed pen, flaming red
Over the ice-blue Atlantic.

I have no fear of flying
No fear of dying. The process,
Yes, the act (if seconds long), Yes.
I wonder, what would I
Say or do during that
Long free fall, the silver
Lure spinning in a power toss
Toward a watery galaxy
Of grave. The cabin filled
With flesh screams careening
Toward a trash pile
Of twisted frame.

Would I look upon these
Strangers then as friends in a
Common end?

Death should be a private affair
Not a mass communion of
Broken bodies floating
Seaward in the salt. . . .

A baby's cry, row 30 aisle,
Breaks the train of talk
That runs behind
My eyes.

I pick a magazine
From the rack,
Glance through *New Yorker*
Quips and cartoons

And ignore the stranger
Next to me.

$\mathcal{P}$OLITICAL CAMPAIGNING is at once enormously invigorating and exhausting. Eighteen- and twenty-hour days are commonplace. Predawn factory-gate appearances, businessmen's breakfasts, high school political science classes, noon-time speeches at service clubs, visits to local factories, a quick tour of Main Street, a coffee at Mrs. Jones's, television interviews for the six o'clock news and a mandatory speech to the annual convention of some group located at least two hundred miles from where you began that morning—this is the menu from which we sup.

In the summer of 1984, I was stuck in the trough of exhaustion and still faced the toughest part of every campaign—the final two months. Diana and I decided that it was time to break away.

While we have covered our state by foot, automobile, airplane and helicopter, we had never enjoyed the experience of sailing up its magnificent coastline.

We packed our bags, grabbed Kevin and Chris (who needed no coaxing) and drove to Southwest Harbor. We rented a glorious boat (along with captain and cook) from Bob and Tina Hinckley and sailed the *Blue Star* north toward Roque Island. For the next three days, we came into contact with whales five miles from shore in a cold and sometimes blustering sea, and with seals sunning themselves on large boulders that are so unmistakably Maine. At night we anchored in harbors and coves that seemed virtually untouched by human hands.

The daytime exhilaration of riding the wind slipped

into evenings of tranquillity under the dark night sheet of infinity. Here we were reminded of the utter brevity of our lives, the insignificance of our anxieties and the absolute duty we had to preserve the power and glory of this earth for future generations.

Blue Star

Blue Star,
   how many have known
   the wind in your sails,

The rhythm of soft swells
   That carry you free
Into the sea, into an
   hourless kind of time?

Or caught the sun
   sliding behind cotton clouds
And shadows turning
   granite shores into
Water color browns?

Have they sighted
   a sudden break in the waves,
A whale blow, a gleaming
   moving rock,

Or dark, sleek seals
   slipping from view
Playing hide and seek
   in the windows of the heart?

Did they anchor
   in a mirrored harbor
   gold with the end of day,

And explore pathless islands
   where lichens, the color
   of four seasons,
   cling to everything?

Were they struck
   by the majesty
   of all the spruce
Old soldiers unfelled,
Standing tall and silent
Lest they stir
   and break the spell?

And when all the sounds of day
   were as dead as stone,
Did they listen to the moon moan
And gaze at the jewels
Strung across the velvet
Neck of night?

Oh, Blue Star,
   a full sail, a gull wing
a sun-filled wave
all merged for us
   into One.

We have known.
We have known.

And the memory
   lingers forever
   in the fathoms
   of
   our
   souls.

Part Six

IN THE WINTER of 1984, I met with poets Andrei Voznesenski and Yevgeny Yevtushenko in their dachas in Peredelkino, just outside of Moscow.

Voznesenski, an artist as well as an architect, was quiet and undemonstrative, but it was easy to detect in him an immense passion for words and world events. "How," he had asked, "can we bring about a more sane relationship between our countries? We cannot permit things to continue as they are. We must make a better effort to understand each other's history and culture." It was a plea for tolerance and restraint in a world that has been miniaturized by technology.

Yevtushenko is a tall, raw-boned man, full of passion and more than a touch of theater. We spent an entire afternoon at his dining-room table over food and wine, talking politics, reciting poetry and discussing how important it was to break down the barriers that so bitterly divide our countries. At one point he said, "Whatever the relationship between our governments, we must continue to meet and talk. Otherwise we will forget each other's faces." It was a statement that reinforced Voznesenski's. Human exchanges will not serve to prevent an act of madness or miscalculation (one is mindful of the pact between Hitler and Stalin), but the absence of contact and communication will surely make it easier for each nation to engage in invective, accusation and chauvinistic chest pounding. In such an atmosphere each country may be better prepared to wage war, but, perhaps, less inclined to prevent it.

I did not think I would see either Voznesenski's or

Yevtushenko's face again, but an invisible thread of friendship had been established. A year later, Paul Winter, a well-known musician, came to see me in Washington. He is a jazz ecologist who travels around the world, recording the sounds of wolves, whales, and seals and then musically emulates their sounds, transporting them into beautiful, exotic symphonies.

Paul wanted to gain access to a remote part of Siberia (a redundancy) to record the sounds of wildlife there as a part of a series of albums to be called *The Song of Russia*. Yevtushenko had sent him to see me with the hope that I could help penetrate the Soviet bureaucracy!

Several months later, I received in the mail a copy of an album entitled *Sun Singer*. It contains some of the most beautiful and haunting melodies I have ever heard.

For Paul Winter

Sun Singer

Quarter the moon
  until it disappears.

Burn the black
  from the deep night hours

So the stars
  may fall to silent sleep.

Set the morning sea
  on fire,

Defy the leadened shoes
  of gravity

And run along
  the rimless pyre

Of the noon-day's
  yellow eye.

Hear the sun singer's
  haunting notes

that play like dolphins
  upon the soul.

O, liquid gold,
  fill my eyes

Drop by drop
  until they turn

Into blind
  ingots

Then let me go,
  sightless into empty lots

Begging still
  for the light.

Unspoken

The word not spoken
goes not quite unheard.

It lingers in the eye,
in the semi-arch of brow.

A gesture of the hand
speaks pages more than words,

The echo rests in the heart
as driftwood does in sand,

To be rubbed by Time
until it rots or shines.

The word not spoken
touches us as music
does the mind.

Deng's Revolution

China,

Of one seed
but two minds,
divided in soul
each seeking to
be whole.

The world watched
fascinated and frightened
by a dragon feeding
upon itself,

A revolutionary age
that chewed its
books and bones in
a blood-running rage.

Let peace unfold
for all to see,
white bloom of
the peach tree.

Let your vision
for prosperity
whisper to the world
without violence and low,
like the wind
in wheat fields.

Part Seven

January Time

January Time,
Panes go blind
With frost,
crystal cataracts.

Chimneys blow blue
While people walk
heads bowed, determined
not to talk,
against the wind.

Winter lays heavy
Upon the land,
White, cold and long.

Summer Night

A summer night sighs,
warm and lazy.

The stars flash smiles
in their happy galaxies.

Fireflies fill the air
with light soliloquies.

Crickets drown time
in their chatter until,

Until a quiet comes
just before dawn.

A silence darker,
darker even than death.

A silence so deep
it becomes a sound.

Then the sun breaks red,
the trees come alive again,

Their long limbs bouncing
with a melody of song.

Just Before

Dusk comes.

The moon hangs high and light,
a stone rubbed white
and wafer thin
by the sun.

The sky is split
into layered geometrics
of soft colors that run
all variants of red.

Lake water turns
mystically into mirrored glass,
even the winged water bugs
suddenly seem too weary
or too terrified to leap.

A quiet seeps in,
a stillness so deep,
just before the night wind
shifts the world
into shadow,
just before the crickets
wax their legs and orchestrate
for the chorus of fireflies
that sing in octaves of light.

And then,
a loon breaks into flight
low across the lake
naked to a killer's eye
until it sinks into
the dark line of tree shadows.

A hoot comes,
an echo in reverse,
lonely as that
cry for man
that came rolling once
from some dark corner
or crack in the universe.

Before all time began.

October

October,
    After the visitors
    have gone to
    asphalt days,

    And highways are
    free of stickered vans
    all the way to
    the sea-bruised
    shore,

You save your
    secret treasure
For those who stay
    to see the first frost
    on ravaged fields,
    and leaves that bleed
    to glory and to death,

Teasing us
    with summer's
    breath,
    with buds that swell again
    in the false hearth

We are not deceived.

Like misers, we count
    the days as if made
    of gold,

And rejoice,
    knowing all the while
    the coming of the cold.

Part Eight

Part Eight

ONCE WHILE DRIVING on the interstate highway, Diana made the observation that the crows seemed to be getting bigger and fatter each year and that the automobile was responsible. Technology was making Nature's task far too easy. She wondered whether the comfort they now enjoyed had killed their work ethic as well. Could they survive the loss of Persian Gulf oil?

Free Lunch

Black crow
what makes you proud,
launching flights like
some blacktop buzzard
along the paved roads,
waiting for man's loud machines
to do your bidding
and flatten the food
that you have no heart
to challenge while it moves?

Cry your ragged cry
fatten your oil-slick body
and grow big.
Pretend through your caw
that you survive on
courage and cunning,
but Black crow know
that man through his artifice
has made you big and powerless,

Know that a time
will come to pass
when his convenience
will no longer serve your will,
engines will cough dry as bone
and the roads revert to grass.

In the darkness of that hour
perched like a fat figurine
upon a pole or yielding pine,

Know that what was free
was not without cost:
You paid for ease
with what you lost.

IN 1962, I was a student at Boston University Law School and Diana was working as a secretary in an office near Boston's Chinatown. We lived on Beacon Hill in a small apartment on Myrtle Street, which offered the quaint feature of a bathroom across the hall.

We did not own a car at the time, so I would walk Diana, who was pregnant with Kevin, partway to work each day through the Boston Common, a beautifully manicured park that is filled with pigeons and more than a few homeless men and women.

Wracked with doubt about whether I would ever survive my first year of law school, apprehensive about the responsibilities associated with parenthood, unsure of what star, if any, would guide our future, I thought often about the pigeons and paupers of Beacon Hill.

Thoughts Stir

(1)

An old man sits bent
on a park bench,
bundled in a ragged coat,

Wearing unwillingly
an unshaven and sad face
that knows the depths
of loss and disregard.

He was a prince once
at birth, I thought,
new and soft and full
of promise, the center
of his family's eye.

But youth, somewhere, along the
way
had fled, his soul had bled
into so many rejection slips.

Broken by most accounts
he huddles there in the cold
flanked by a legion of pigeons
that squabble and flutter
about his feet, begging
for that which he had
none to give.

How short the fall
from prince to pauper
from hope to husk,

How short the Time.

(2)

Frost climbs the window
with crystal intricacy and design
while the mercury drops
into the wide bulb
at the base of spine.

The moon is bright
and brittle. The stars
cascade in shimmering
galaxies, tinkling into Time.

Thoughts stir
in my mind
like dark roots
struggling to penetrate
the soil in another
season.

They reach no conclusion.

(3)

On the ledge outside my room,
a pigeon perches in silence
seeking asylum against the cold,
looking down at all
the fleeting lights
from cars that are indifferent
as the night's high stars.

It just sits there,
asking not for recognition
or understanding or mercy,
just warmth in the darkness
of another hour.

(4)

Will I ever reach
that purity of being
beyond ambition and hope
of some indefinable goal

So that I might live
and pass away
the way wild things die,
quietly, without question,
without answer, without anguish,

Satisfied that I am
but a part of a process
that I cannot explain
nor feel compelled to understand,
but unthinking understand?

(5)

Thoughts stir in my mind.
They reach no conclusion.

IN AUGUST 1979, Diana and I were invited to join eighteen Maine citizens on a "mission" to Israel. We arrived in Tel Aviv and began a journey to a small nation that contains an incredible mixture of all that is modern and much that is old.

We headed south to Gaza and visited the Palestinian refugee camps. While the camps were not nearly as bleak as I had expected, most Americans would not consider the living conditions there acceptable. What seemed to break the curse for the victims of war were hundreds of Palestinian children who kept running after our bus, waving to all of us. Their eyes looked like pools of chocolate syrup, their smiles as dazzling as fresh flowers.

We spent four days traveling up the west coast of Israel under the skillful tutelage of our guide, Zvika Gerstel, whose speech was as rich and lyrical as any poet's I have ever known. Then we were off to the Golan Heights to visit with Israeli soldiers whose eyes never quite left the horizon or the distant valley.

Finally, we arrived in Jerusalem. The sight of the Old City—the walls that have endured so many assaults, the rocks and relics of the past scattered on the hills like dinosaurs' teeth that have gone yellow in the sun—was simply breathtaking. Here the three great religions of the world converged and stood star-crossed, powerful, poignant and destructive. At night, you could stand by the walls of Solomon and in the silence hear voices from another age. Crucifixion, Crusades and Holocaust took on a deeper significance than we had ever known. At Yad Vashem, the memorial to the

Holocaust, we saw evidence of a brutality that surpassed the limits of human imagination. For me, it was not the horror of the ovens being stoked with living corpses that clutched my throat, not the masses of skin-covered skeletons being bulldozed into uncovered graves like so much refuse. It was the sight of a young boy wearing a cap and short coat that covered just the top of his knees. He was standing with his hands raised above his head while a Nazi soldier held a rifle to his back. In that young boy's eyes I could see not terror, but all that brown sadness that man has ever known.

It was then that I understood why the eyes of the Israeli soldiers on the Golan Heights were always cast outward, always on alert.

For Zvika

We came
on a pilgrimage of sorts,
strangers tracing in time
the paths of wandering tribes
over the hills of Judea
to the gates of Palestine.

Four thousand years
dissolved in the desert heat.
History was compressed
between the lips
of our guide
into the moving
mosaic of his mind.

Only eight days,
eight candles of light.
But time enough
to think of time
and towns that lay
in layers of broken stone
and powdered lime,

And feel the soft
shuffle of our fathers' feet
in the pale desert
of the Promised Land.

Time to witness
the miracles of trees
shouting green
in the Sinai's sand,
and Arab children
waving smiles like
lilies in the sun.

To stand at Caesarea
on the reconstructed stage
of King Herod's dark days
and catch, in the silence
between the waves,
just an echo of
ancient Roman plays.

To see Haifa
rise up from the sea
and spiral, it seemed,
into clouds of cumulus
like a young girl's dream.

Time to taste the fruit
from valleys made fertile
by black, hot rocks
blown from the bellies
of angry hills.

Valleys that have
run red too
with the blood
of all the Jews
who stood and died
before their time
under the Star of David.

Gaza, Golan, Galilee.
Jaffa, Judea, Jericho,
their lyrics climb
like ivy in the heart
until they touch
the memory of Romans,
Crusades and Holocaust.

Then the pain comes
and moves across the mind
like black-robed Bedouins,
phantoms that pick
the desert of its growth,
and leave the sand exposed.

Yad Vashem,
the haunting photographs
of Abraham's children
sheared like sheep,
thrown as bones
to the dogs of hell,
tattoo our souls
with their epitaphs . . .

    Remember.

Talk is again of peace
even as the air
rings with the hammer
striking steel.

The cry is for the Jews
to be just, once more,
and shrink back to borders
that invited war.

For what purpose
does the hammer ring?
Is it a time
to mourn or a time to sing?

The steel's edge
is razor thin.
It may be a scythe.
It may be a sword.

So young men
with restless eyes
sit high on
the heights and sigh,
    "We only want to live.
    Masada, Treblinka, Auschwitz
    shall never be again."

And they wait
for the answer
in the wind.
But the wind's whisper
is too low for now.

So they sit and watch
with weapons cocked
and measure each bird
that flies alone or in flock.

They wait for the wind
to touch the trees
and sing a hymn,

        "This year Peace.
        This year in Jerusalem."

Henry Jackson

(1912–1983)

O, gentle warrior,
you who hung
a winged sentry
above your doubting
countrymen,

And warned of violence
ticking away
in the margins of our indifference,

How, as the days
dropped into decades,
did you always come
armed with but words
and wise intelligence

Knowing that the
issue of the hour
was never lost or won,
but rejoiced, unbroken,
by the battle
the hour had brung?

Suns perish, moons fade,
bodies more sublime
than we have been
taken by Time to eternity.

But you,
uncursed as Cain,
were too vigorous to die,
no, not of a bursting heart
that never once
had bothered to complain

And yet,
a square-cut stone
now will mark
for all to see
the residence that
you've taken
in the village
of cold mortality.

I write these words,
toss this voweled wreath
upon your resting place
mindful, even as
I feed upon
the bitter salt
of grief,

That once,
as a boy,
I watched in
wonderment and joy
a heavenly meteor
drop to death
in a brilliant
slash of light.

So your spirit
remains with me,
burning intense and bright,
forever in my memory,

As you fall
silent now,
blazing
into
the
vastness
of
the
night.

The Stargazers

The night
drowns in the silence
of the stars;

Light breaks
like blown glass
upon a shrouded street;

An explosion
tears the ear of heaven
but makes no sound;

A scream
falls, a burning arrow
across the blackened galaxy;

And we,
impaled with wonder,
weep at the majesty
of this distant death.

Princeton Conference

Jack boots, goose steps,
a haunting specter
rises from the ashes,
takes form as echoes
ripple inside my ears.

Thirty years since
the roar of ovens—
Treblinka, Bergen-Belsen, Dachau—
the telling tattoo, dog tag
of the Jew.
The stench of human flesh
rotting in its home of open
graves
is recalled from the
bank of chromosomes.

There's no gold in my smile
my skin is not fit
for shades, my . . .

But today, I sit in conference:
"Mr. Cohen, meet Mr.
von Weizsacher."
It's all quite civilized
and proper,
discussing trade and technology
over coffee and tea.

Time heals. The scars of war
have been rubbed with trade.
We are friends, now, bonded
in defense against
a larger enemy.

But do they see
the flick of fear
in my eyes
at the click
of an accent.

In one of the coldest days in the winter of 1984, Diana, with a picture-perfect swing, cracked the bow of a new 688 class attack submarine with a bottle of champagne. She named the ship AUGUSTA (whether because it is our state's capital or her birthplace I have never dared to inquire). It went slipping down the ways into the icy Connecticut River with our sons standing topside and a Navy band playing "Anchors Aweigh."

Nearly a year later, the AUGUSTA sailed to the Portsmouth-Kittery shipyard, where she was officially commissioned. It was nearly as cold as the day of her birth and a snowfall kept the official speeches relatively brief. I read this poem at the conclusion of my remarks.

Mighty AUGUSTA

Mighty AUGUSTA,
indifferent to wind or wave,
sail-less, set sail,
under the gaze
of lovely Diana.

Slip now,
beneath the cold sea
into sunless days
when even noon
is dark as night.

Deep into
that dark, where
wondrous creatures
hidden to the eye
live in violent anonymity.

Move there silently
as night clouds
move across the moon
and leave no tracks.

Sleepless, through
your green eye
search the vast waters
for those who
mean us harm;
save your poised fury
O silent sentinel,
for only our enemies.

And when the months
dissolve into years
and you weary
of your task,

think of the pine tree
straight and proud,
think of the moose
moving easily
among the woods
and sweet song
of the chickadee.

And know that
through your night-filled
days of sacrifice,

We of Maine and America
remain the children of liberty.

Part Nine

Part Nine

Adonis

How their eyes
once turned
when in his youth
he strode.

How fire then burned
in their soft-sweatered
breasts,

And blood did pound
inside their veins
with crimson thoughts
of love and lust.

How he did take pleasure
in the sorrow
of their silent pain

And laughed his laugh
inside his heart
at their exquisite agony.

But swiftly as the stars
flash their smiles at night
then fade in yellow dawn,
so Time did shift its course.

And now he sits
alone and bent
beside his stove,

Listening to ashes
sift through the
fingered grates,

Thinking, how foolish
was pride's flattery,
How quickly did beauty
become a memory.

Emerson Insight

The poet's back
seems so often
to be without
brawn.

The reason no doubt
he turns his hand to song
and hews words
instead of wood
with the cutting
edge of tongue.

So the fox,
small in terms of girth,
knows his amber worth
rests not on strength but wile
and thus escapes
the hound's angry tooth
by cultivating guile.

And too the blind man
whose eyes are
filled with night
hears sounds and secrets
amplified to heights
beyond those who profess
to see with their sight.

The mystery of life's force
flows like water
to a determined level
and when diverted
from its course,
by accident or birth,
seeks to compensate,
and reallocates plenty
where there was dearth.

The Myth of Er

I struck a match
  And watched it burn—a body
Torn from the roll call of oblivion
And suddenly given life by
  An indifferent hand.

The flame flickered bright with
sporadic
Vigor and seemed as if some surges
Would go unbridled, but the

Spirit slowly receded
  And the fire humbly mellowed
Until the spine was gray and bent,
And a silent cry of smoke was wafted
into

                    the

                          star-filled
                            night.

Versification of Frost

There's a vigorous devil
inside my soul
that plots a course
first above, then below
the level of remorse.

Sometimes sorrow weeps internally
but not as much
as when the wind's cold touch
prompts a tear externally.

There Is Time

If I were old
I'd spend each day
polishing my soul
until it gleamed white
with wisdom and with
truth.

At the risk
of being labeled mad,
I'd tug on the tails
of Spring and beg
Summer not to leave.
Even Winter I'd befriend
and bless the day
snow would bury hay,
yes, I'd even ask the cold
to stay.

But I am a young man
only thirty, you see,
and there is time
enough for me,
to pray for time.

Hourglass

Tonight, while sitting
in my opulent chair,
I found loneliness hanging
just above despair.

There were piles of paper work,
the rhythm of radiowaves
and the quiet exchange
of sleeping children muffled
in quilted octaves.

Night trebled
the sound of cold rain
pounding on the windowpane,
copper pipes clicked and clanged
and desperate thoughts
linked themselves together
in a heavy, rattling chain.

I was alone
in a crowd of sound
listening for your voice
through the wall
of a distant town.

Is this how death comes
to a household at last,
in wind and rain
and the amplified pain
of ice cubes melting
in a bourbon hourglass?

Where intangible fears
flutter through empty rooms
like blind phantom bats,
and every tomorrow is filled
with gossamer thoughts
of a golden love forever lost?

Come back.
Take me from this night
and make me whole again.

A Berryman Delusion

It is morning again. The
sun is streaking through glass,
birds are playing happy notes
through valved lutes. . . . The
sounds of life that slept
under evening's sheet
are blinking awake.

Shower, shave, blue shirt,
what color tie?
Hurry, senses, there's a list
and lots of things
to be done.
Have you seen my shoes?

There, I'm together now,
prepared for battle and debate,
ready now to welcome friends
to undo those holding me in hate
I am prepared. . . .

Wait!
Prepared for what?
Oh, doubt erupts into riot everywhere
attacking me on the stairs,
ancient furies beat decaying wings
shrieking out the sound of my thoughts.
I am no reader of lips.

Mission dissolves into mockery
laughter turns to leer,
in a flash, a phantasmagoric moment,
I have fallen from command into a coma
of doubt,
a man torn and tortured within,
what avenue out can I take?

My sons appear at their
bedroom doors, pushed from sleep,
preparing to meet the same sun,
shielding their own fears under
innocence.

Tiger is to be fed. Lunch money paid,
a soccer practice tonight.
"Dad, I don't know how to divide . . ."

They have their battles to win.

Diana, in full bloom now,
sinking roots into
deeper soil, art and ballet,
she grows taller each day.

Eggs are breaking, bacon frying,
I'm back. That scream across
the canyon left as soon as
its echo rippled out.

I do not know for what
I am preparing or prepared,
but I am redeemed and
whole again, knowing that
I have been, now am,
without mission, perhaps mercy,

but with health
and the succoring
love of a family.

Clara's Eyes

What passions are aroused
when bloodlines are crossed
and run into veins
that cannot account
for the loss
of innocence?

How many years
you held your golden head
high in silence,

Amid those whispers
and jaundiced looks,
the epithets hurled
at the flesh of your flesh
that struck like stones.

There was no harbor,
no sanctuary, not
in the ranks of Christ or
Maccabee
for being half of each
they fell beyond
the reach of conformity.

Did you weaken ever once?
Did you ever wonder whether
it was worth it all
to be neither Jew nor Gentile?

No. I think not.
You stood tall and firm
against all the subtle
exclusions, knowing
the alloy was stronger
than the ore.

Knowing that love,
the pride inside
your Irish eyes
would be wall enough.

It was. We go on,
scarred but strong.

And grateful beyond words.

Indian Point

Here on the coast of Maine
where rocks are pounded
by sleepless Atlantic tides,
I have time to contemplate
away from the acrimony and debate
that fill my days.

Time to watch black ducks float
serenely on icy waters and
then suddenly lurch beneath
the surface in search
of some moving thing;

Time to see lobstermen
circle in the fog
dumping and hauling pots
in constant pattern and pursuit of
their clawed catch,
while sandpipers scurry about
like some tiny regiment or band
along the edge of each new wave
picking their food from the bubbling sand.

There is a harmony
to this unending struggle
even in the fog
that sweeps in and softens in gauze
the sound of bells and haunting horns.

It is a place of ripples and reflections,
an ancient asylum
of quiet echoes from
another age.

And yet, amid this peace,
before my heart is healed
and the acid drains
from my veins,
I burn for the fever,
the intolerable pace
where passions pristine
teem and boil in transcripted words
and each day begins and ends
in some small compromise
that is cut in the name
of consensus.

The man of passion
cannot be appeased with peace.
A candle, he is complete
only when he burns.

A Christmas Greeting*

Peace,
      Joy,
            Good
                  Will.

The words cascade
like a sunset's shillings
into a cup of gold
that we hold
in our hearts.

And they glow there
for those who know
the power of love
and feel the flower
of friendship.

*Written for Joy Baker's Christmas card.

Love's Fickle Ear

If Time should come
when I am old
and wrinkled white,

If Beauty should despair
its wreckage upon the rocks
of broken dreams

And curse the unkind light
that floods the room
without remorse,

Shall I then repair
with soft memories
of youth's passions and mistakes
that scorned wisdom's offerings
and stoned it with malice
as a child might a ragged man?

Or know, instead, that life
spent on art and symphonies
refining old philosophies
could not appease
the body's strife
or make the end
less cruel?

The young are destined
to whisper into Love's
fickle ear,

The old to rejoice
in the knowledge
of their years.

And me . . . to stand
a dry stick
rubbing my words together,
striking no sparks.

Part Ten

Aboard the Missing Papers

The poet says:
    "A word caught
    can make a world
    appear."

What word
    trapped in ink
can catch a sail
in the wind,
the white wing
of a gull hanging
on the edge of the sea
on fire suddenly
with the sun's
dancing gold?

What syllable
    falling on the ear
Can match the beauty
of stars flung across
the infinity of night,

Of one that dies
and falls into a brilliant
screaming agony of light
yet yields no sound?

What song
    floating on a scale
can sing of a Caribbean
first ice blue
then aqua green
once savage
now serene

of young dolphins
playing at our bow,
and magic fish
and corals beneath
painted by a laughing child?

What melody
lingering in the heart
can speak of pelicans
climbing to a point
hovering, fluttering until
they drop, as if shot,
dead into a wave,
emerging with just
a flash of meek silver
wiggling in their beaks?

What rhyme
        played in pentameters
can describe the
blueness of the sky
measure the tranquillity
of nautical time

Or tell how
        fleckless and free
is the spirit
finally shorn of bodies
we've worn like
proud and heavy crowns?

Alone, at last, at sea
our tongues turn to wood
our vowels to stone.

In the absence of words
there remains the experienc

And the memory.

Blessing of the Fleet

The leaf will go from
green to gold,
years will slip
into Time.

But still the vast waters
will shine and roar

Changing the earth's pattern
infinitely and forever.

The sea calls,
moans its haunting moan

To a hearty few

And washes the moon
with its night-dimmed tide.

Come, the morning's on fire
The waves gleam and roll

The gulls are crying,

O fisherman, fisherman
Safe be thy soul.

Blue Heaven

At last,
the fog lifts,
the sun breaks
and clouds turn
into dove feathers
that fan the light
until the sky is
soul-blinding blue.

And the blue
bleeds into layered
shades that sink
into the sea
until the sky
and sea are one
and the horizon
is but a thin
thread of thought
stretched across
my mind.

Leather creaks
with the rhythm
of an old rocking chair
as I rock high
on a proud and gentle horse
from Tennessee
that carries me
as a woman might
a rose.

Up here, where
a giant fist of ice
once pounded its way
into hills gone green
with life,

Where the hawk hangs
watchful and fierce
and the silence
is broken by a
dog's lonely bark,

The memory—
of the wind,
the taste of salt
and hoofs splashing
on the wave-wounded shore—
is fixed forever
like a birthmark
on my heart.

Close to Eden

(For Dan & Jean)
(Pete & Judi)

Autumn again.
Leaves, the texture
of skins shed,
their colors bled
from a rainbow,
fall in a whisper
from the wind
into a coat
of red and gold
that floats
on a pond damned
to a stillness
clear as glass.

Alas, the wheel of Time
has spun,
trees stand nude
against the sun
that hangs low
now against the
afternoon hour.

From here
one can see
young deer
walking at ease
blending with trees
while city sounds
go deferred;

The hearth is warm
with burning logs
and laughter greets
the passing of spiced wine,

The agonies of war
and men gone mad
do not echo here,
not in this cove
of respite and repair.

To know
and yet to go
beyond the knowing;
to feel friendship
grow tight as vines
as we give grace,
our voices merging
with the calm.

This as close
as one can come
to Eden.

ABOUT THE AUTHOR

William S. Cohen, Republican of Maine, served three terms in the U.S. House of Representatives before being elected to the Senate in 1978. Cohen is a member of the Armed Services and Governmental Affairs committees, as well as the Special Committee on Aging and the Select Committee on Intelligence. He is the author of three other books: *Of Sons and Seasons* (poetry), *Roll Call*, and *Getting the Most Out of Washington*. He is also co-author with Senator Gary Hart of the thriller novel *The Double Man*.